CONTENTS

Be A Word Detective 5

Chapter 1
THE OCEAN 6

Chapter 2
OCEAN PLANTS 13

Chapter 3
OCEAN PLANT EATERS 20

Chapter 4
OCEAN MEAT EATERS 24

Chapter 5
OCEAN DECOMPOSERS 31

Chapter 6
PEOPLE AND THE OCEAN 36

A Note to Adults on Sharing a Book 44

Learn More about Oceans and Food Webs 45

Glossary 46

Index 48

An Ocean Food Web

giant kelp

northern kelp crab

sea urchin

herring

sea otter

gull

octopus

killer whale

OCEAN
FOOD WEBS

BY PAUL FLEISHER

LERNER BOOKS ••• MINNEAPOLIS

The photographs in this book are used with the permission of: © John Foxx/Stockbyte/Getty Images, backgrounds on pp. 1, 6, 13, 20, 24, 31, 36, 45, 46, 47; Courtesy of Larry Benvenuti, National Oceanic and Atmospheric Administration Central Library Photo Collection, p. 5; Courtesy of NOAA, p. 6; © Reinhard Dirsherl/Visuals Unlimited, pp. 7, 33, 47; © PHONE Gohier François/Peter Arnold, Inc., p. 9; © David Wrobel/Visuals Unlimited, pp. 10, 13, 21, 25; © S. E. Arndt/Peter Arnold, Inc., p. 11; © Fritz Polking/Peter Arnold, Inc., p. 12; © Hal Beral/Visuals Unlimited, p. 15; © altrendo travel/Getty Images, p. 16; © Konrad Wothe/ Look/Getty Images, p. 17; © Chuck Davis/Stone/Getty Images, p. 18; © Peter David/Taxi/Getty Images, p. 19; © Daniel W. Gotshall/Visuals Unlimited, p. 20; © Glenn Oliver/Visuals Unlimited, p. 22; © Brandon Cole Marine Photography/Alamy, p. 23; © John Seagrim/Taxi/ Getty Images, p. 24; © Richard Herrmann/Visuals Unlimited, p. 26; © David McNew/Peter Arnold, Inc., p. 27; © Mike Anich/Visuals Unlimited, p. 28; © Marty Snyderman/Visuals Unlimited, p. 29; © Aldo Brando/Stone/Getty Images, p. 30; © Paul Nicklen/National Geographic/Getty Images, p. 31; © Paolo Curto/The Image Bank/Getty Images, p. 32; © SAS/Alamy, p. 34; © Michael Nichols/National Geographic/Getty Images, p. 35; © Wolfgang Poelzer/Peter Arnold, Inc., p. 36; © Stuart Paton/The Image Bank/Getty Images, p. 37; © DEA/M. BERTINELLI/De Agostini Picture Library/Getty Images, p. 38; © Ullstein-Teich/Peter Arnold, Inc., p. 39; © BIOS Borrell Bartomeu/Peter Arnold, Inc., p. 40; © Leroy Simon/Visuals Unlimited, p. 41; © Ray Pfortner/Peter Arnold, Inc., p. 42; © Jeff Greenberg/Peter Arnold, Inc., p. 43; Courtesy of Mike White, NOAA's Coral Kingdom Collection, p. 46; Courtesy of the Florida Keys National Marine Sanctuary Staff, NOAA's Coral Kingdom Sanctuary; p. 48 Illustrations on pp. 4, 14 by Zeke Smith, © Lerner Publishing Group, Inc.; map on p. 8 © Laura Westlund/Independent Picture Service.
Cover: © David Wrobel/Visuals Unlimited (top); © Richard Herrmann/Visuals Unlimited (bottom left); Courtesy of Florida Keys National Marine Sanctuary, part of the NOAA Central Library Photo Collection (bottom right); © John Foxx/Stockbyte/Getty Images (background).

Early Bird Food Webs series diagrams created by Zeke Smith.

First published in the United Kingdom in 2008 by
Lerner Books,
Dalton House,
60 Windsor Avenue,
London SW19 2RR

Website address: www.lernerbooks.co.uk

This edition was updated and edited for UK publication by Discovery Books Ltd., Unit 3, 37 Watling Street, Leintwardine, Shropshire SY7 0LW

British Library Cataloguing in Publication Data

Fleisher, Paul
Ocean food webs. - (Early bird food chains)
1. Marine ecology - Juvenile literature 2. Food chains (Ecology) - Juvenile literature
I. Title
577.7

ISBN-13: 978 1 58013 472 9

Printed in China

BE A WORD DETECTIVE

Can you find these words as you read about ocean food webs? Be a detective and try to work out what they mean. You can turn to the glossary on page 46 for help.

algae	decomposers	nutrients
bacteria	environment	omnivores
carnivores	food chain	photosynthesis
consumers	food web	plankton
decay	herbivores	producers

This is what the Earth looks like from space. The green parts are land. What are the blue areas?

CHAPTER 1
THE OCEAN

From space, our world looks mostly blue. Look at a globe. Most of the globe is blue. The blue parts are water. Almost three-quarters of the world is covered with ocean.

Most water on the Earth is ocean water. Ocean water is salty. It is too salty to drink, but it is

Creatures of all sizes live in the ocean. Some are tiny. Others are very big. Whales live in the ocean, they are the biggest animals on Earth.

Fish swim in the ocean. Worms burrow in the mud of the ocean floor. Clams live in the mud too. Crabs crawl along the bottom. Seabirds fly above the water. Many creatures live along the coastline.

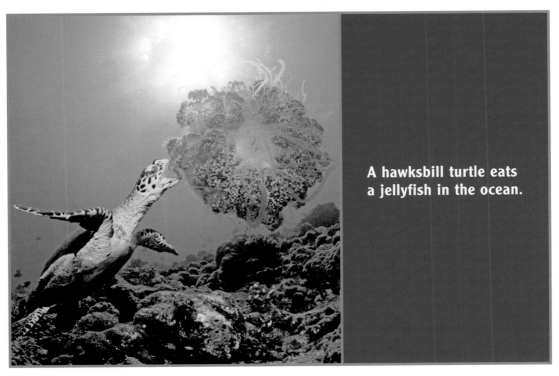

A hawksbill turtle eats a jellyfish in the ocean.

The ocean is a very important environment. An environment is a place where any creature lives. The ocean environment includes the air, water, sand or mud, and weather. It includes other plants and animals too.

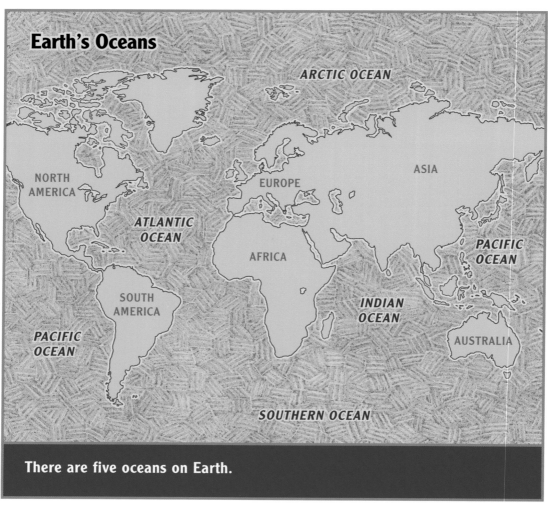

Earth's Oceans

ARCTIC OCEAN

ASIA

NORTH AMERICA

EUROPE

ATLANTIC OCEAN

PACIFIC OCEAN

AFRICA

SOUTH AMERICA

INDIAN OCEAN

PACIFIC OCEAN

AUSTRALIA

SOUTHERN OCEAN

There are five oceans on Earth.

Fin whales and seabirds feed on fish called herring. The herring feed on tiny ocean plants and animals.

Living things in the ocean environment depend on one another. They form a web of life. Some animals eat plants. Other animals are meat eaters. Some creatures feed on dead plants and animals. When plants and animals die, they break down into chemicals. The chemicals help other plants grow.

Living things get energy from food. Energy moves from one living thing to another. A food chain shows how the energy moves. The energy for life comes from the sun. The sun's energy is stored in plants. Animals eat the plants. They get some of the sun's energy from the plants. The energy moves along the food chain. When one creature eats another, some of the energy is passed on.

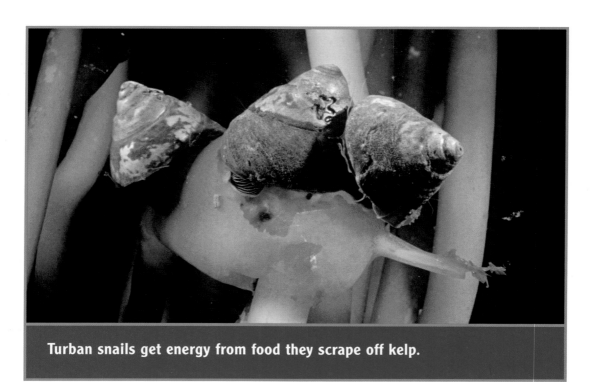

Turban snails get energy from food they scrape off kelp.

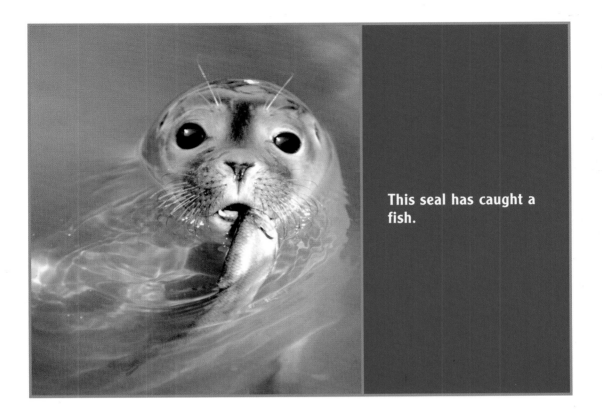

This seal has caught a fish.

There are many food chains in the ocean. Here is one example. A snail eats plants. Then a fish eats the snail. Then a seal eats the fish. When the seal dies, crabs eat its body. Some of the sun's energy goes from the plants to the snail. Then energy is passed to the fish. Then energy goes to the seal. Crabs get energy from the dead seal when they eat its body.

A food web is made of many food chains. Fish eat other things besides snails. They eat prawns. They also eat worms and other fish. Seals eat many different kinds of fish. They eat octopuses and squid too. Crabs feed on all kinds of dead animals and plants. Everything each creature eats is part of a food web. A food web shows how all living things in an environment depend on one another for food.

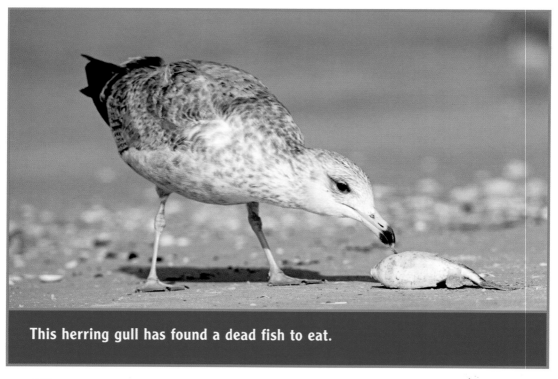

This herring gull has found a dead fish to eat.

Sunlight shines through a giant kelp forest. Kelp and other ocean plants use sunlight to make food. What else do they make?

CHAPTER 2
OCEAN PLANTS

Green plants use sunlight to make food. Living things that make their own food are called producers. Animals use the food that plants produce. Plants also make oxygen. Oxygen is a gas in the air and water. Animals need

Plants make food and oxygen through photosynthesis. Plants need sunlight for photosynthesis. They also need carbon dioxide and water. Carbon dioxide is a gas in the air. It is in the water too. Plants take in carbon dioxide. They take in water. Plants use energy from sunlight to turn water and carbon dioxide into sugar and starch. Sugar and starch are the plants' food. Plants store the food in their bodies. This food helps plants to grow.

Photosynthesis

sunlight

carbon dioxide

oxygen

water

Kelp use sunlight, carbon dioxide and water to make their own food.

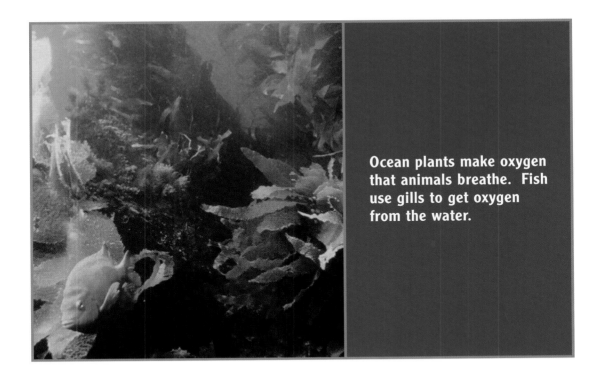

Ocean plants make oxygen that animals breathe. Fish use gills to get oxygen from the water.

Plants also make oxygen as they make food. The oxygen goes into the air and the water. Animals breathe the oxygen. They breathe out carbon dioxide. Plants use the carbon dioxide to make more food.

Water contains chemicals called nutrients. Living things need nutrients to grow. Plants get nutrients when they take in water.

Algae are plants that float in the water. Most algae are too small to see, but huge numbers of algae grow in the ocean. Algae make the water look green.

Some algae are a kind of plankton. Plankton are living creatures that float and drift in the water. Some plankton are producers.

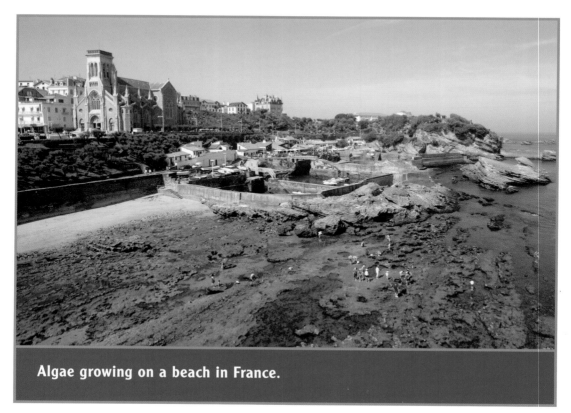

Algae growing on a beach in France.

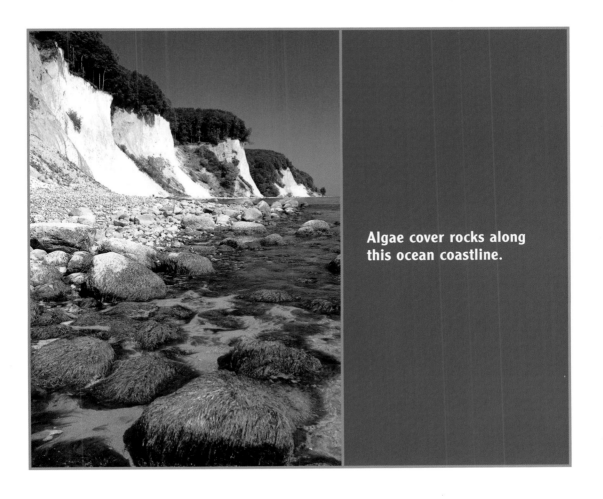

Algae cover rocks along this ocean coastline.

Algae are the most important producers on Earth. Algae make most of the oxygen that animals breathe. Ocean animals also eat algae. Algae need sunlight to grow. Sunlight is brighter near the surface of the ocean. So algae grow only near the surface.

Large algae called seaweed also live in the ocean. Most seaweed grows near the shore. Some seaweed floats on the surface of the ocean.

Blue rockfish swim through a giant kelp forest. Giant kelp is a kind of seaweed. It can grow 30 metres tall!

Strange-looking creatures live in the deep, dark parts of the ocean. This deep-sea angler feeds on other fish. Those fish eat food that drifts down from the surface.

No algae grow in the deep parts of the ocean. Light cannot reach there. The deep waters are dark, but deep-water animals need algae too. They need the oxygen algae make. They depend on the animals that eat the algae.

This northern kelp crab lives and feeds on kelp. What other ocean animals eat plants?

CHAPTER 3
OCEAN PLANT EATERS

Living things that eat other living things are consumers. *Consume* means 'eat'. Animals are consumers.

Animals that eat plants are called herbivores. The sun's energy is stored in the plants. When an animal eats plants, it gets the sun's energy.

Most ocean herbivores are small. Tiny animal plankton float in the ocean. Many animal plankton feed on algae. Small worms, baby clams and prawns eat algae.

Copepods are also a kind of animal plankton. They look like tiny prawns. They eat algae too.

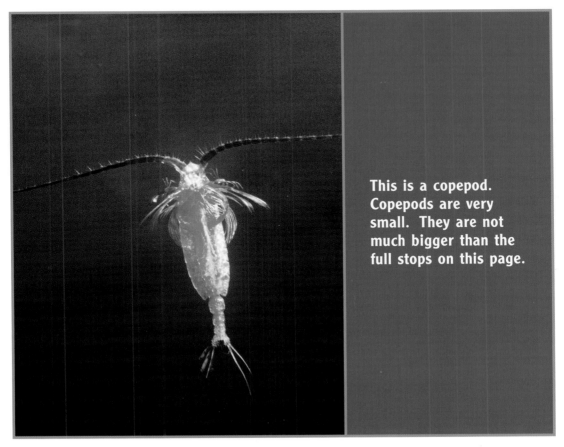

This is a copepod. Copepods are very small. They are not much bigger than the full stops on this page.

Oysters and clams eat algae. They take in water and they strain algae out of it.

Snails scrape algae from rocks to eat. Snails also eat kelp. Sea urchins and kelp crabs feed on kelp.

This clam is taking in water filled with tiny algae.

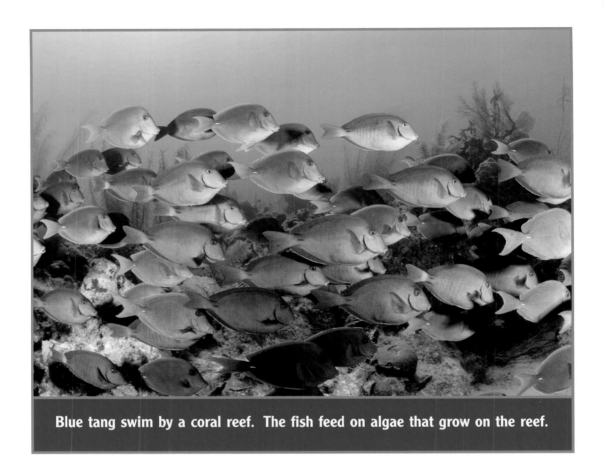

Blue tang swim by a coral reef. The fish feed on algae that grow on the reef.

Some larger animals eat algae. Green sea turtles graze on algae. Some fish eat algae too. Blue tang eat algae growing on coral reefs. Corals are tiny ocean animals that build stony homes. Over many years, the corals' homes pile up to make a rocky reef. Many ocean plants and animals live in and around coral reefs.

Octopuses hunt near the ocean floor for other animals to eat. What are animals that eat meat called?

CHAPTER 4

OCEAN MEAT EATERS

Most ocean animals eat meat. Meat-eating animals are called carnivores. Carnivores catch and eat other animals. Carnivores depend on plants too. Carnivores get energy by eating animals that have eaten plants.

Many ocean animals eat animal plankton. Jellyfish catch plankton in their long, thin tentacles. Sea anemones also catch small animals in their tentacles.

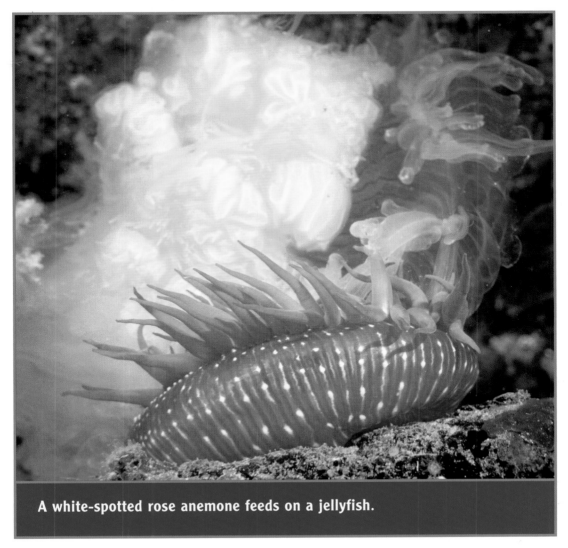

A white-spotted rose anemone feeds on a jellyfish.

Ocean fish eat other animals. Sea bass eat worms and crabs. They also hunt small fish. Bluefish and tuna are fast swimmers. They catch smaller fish to eat. Some sharks eat bluefish and tuna. Sharks also eat octopuses and other large ocean animals.

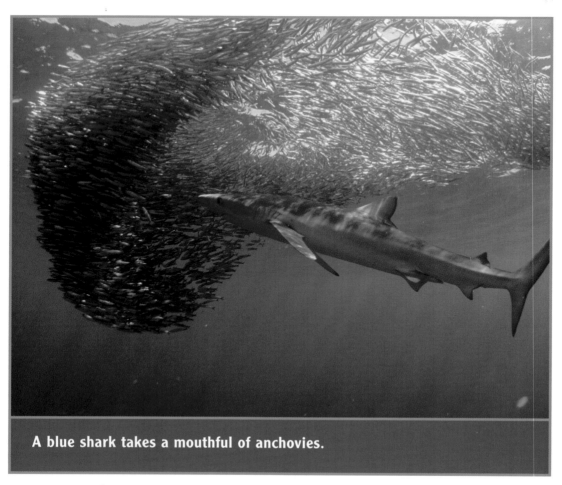

A blue shark takes a mouthful of anchovies.

This seal was almost food for a hungry killer whale.

Octopuses are carnivores. They hunt for crabs. Octopuses eat lobsters too.

Whales are meat eaters. Some whales eat animal plankton. Right whales eat copepods. Killer whales hunt for fish, birds and seals.

Seals and sea otters eat fish. Sea otters
also feed on sea urchins and crabs. Seabirds
also feed on fish. Pelicans dive into the water.
They catch fish in their beaks. Gulls and terns
catch fish too.

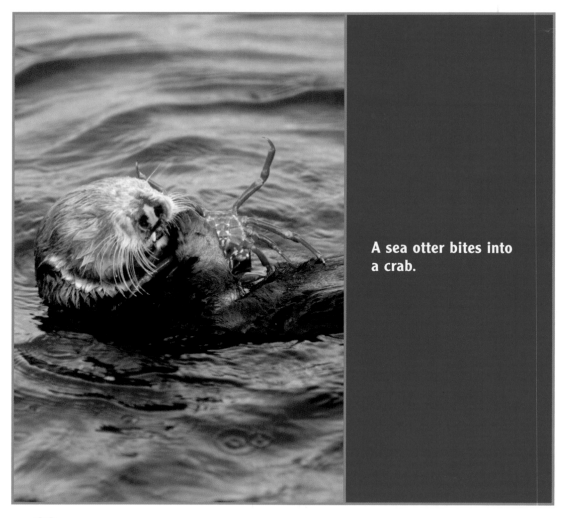

A sea otter bites into
a crab.

A red and black anemone fish hides in a sea anemone. The fish eats algae and copepods near the anemone.

Some consumers eat both plants and animals. These animals are called omnivores. Damselfish are omnivores. Damselfish eat algae. They also eat animal plankton and small, shrimp-like animals.

Some fish gather plankton in their mouths as they swim. These fish are omnivores. They eat both plant and animal plankton. Herring and anchovies swim in large groups with their mouths open, eating the plankton they catch.

Mole crabs are omnivores. Mole crabs burrow in wet sand. They filter the water in the sand to find plankton to eat.

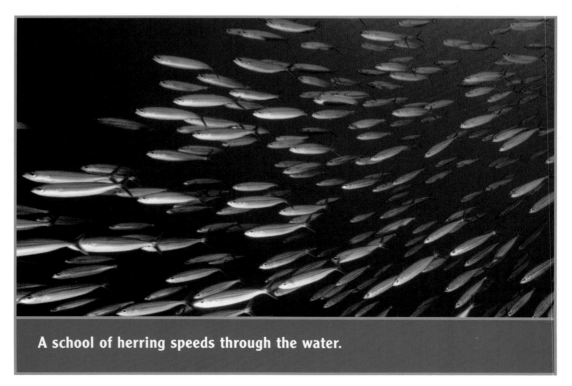

A school of herring speeds through the water.

A dead fish sinks to the bottom of the ocean. What will happen to its body?

CHAPTER 5
OCEAN DECOMPOSERS

All living things die. When plants or animals die, they decay. They break down into nutrients. Living things called decomposers help dead things decay. Decomposers feed on dead creatures.

31

Something has killed a large number of fish in this part of the ocean. Decomposers will break down the bodies into nutrients for algae and other ocean plants.

Decomposers are nature's recyclers. They help break down dead plants and animals. Dead creatures sink to the bottom of the ocean. Decomposers feed on them. The dead plants and animals slowly become part of the sand and mud. Nutrients from them go back into the water. Then other living things can use the nutrients again.

Decomposers are very important. Without them, the ocean would be full of dead plants and animals. Then no new plants could grow. Animals would run out of food.

Some ocean animals are scavengers. They find and eat the bodies of dead animals. Some sharks feed on dead animals floating on the surface of the water. Crabs and lobsters eat dead animals that sink to the bottom.

This lobster has found a meal on the ocean floor.

Sea cucumbers live near the ocean floor. They hold on to rocks or crawl along the sand. Sea cucumbers swallow sand. They eat little bits of dead things in the sand.

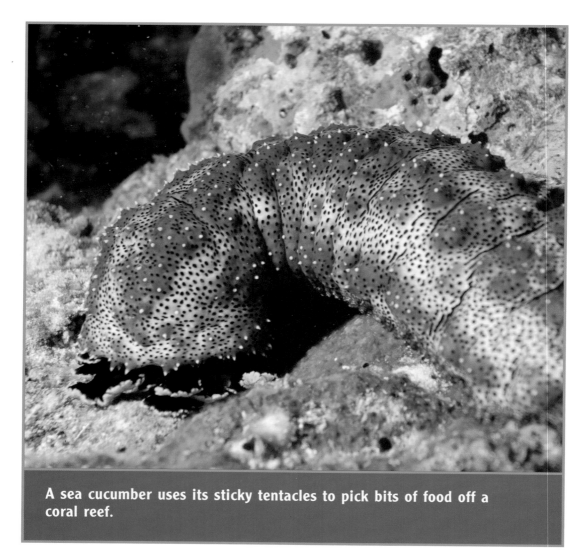

A sea cucumber uses its sticky tentacles to pick bits of food off a coral reef.

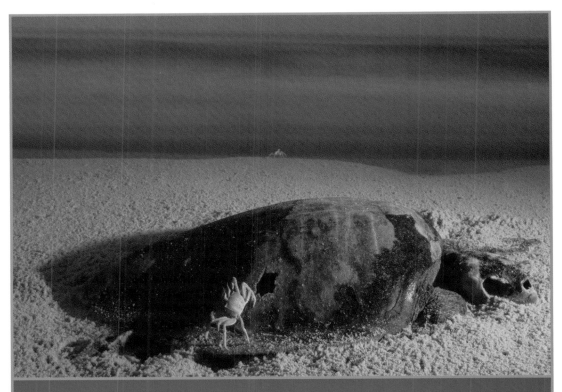

A crab scurries across the body of a dead sea turtle. Crabs and other animals will pick away at the body. Tiny bacteria will break down what is left.

Bacteria are the ocean's most important decomposers. Billions of tiny bacteria live in the water. Billions more live in the mud. Bacteria feed on dead creatures in the water and mud. They break down the creatures into nutrients, which will help ocean plants to grow.

A diver swims near a coral reef. Why do people enjoy the ocean?

CHAPTER 6
PEOPLE AND THE OCEAN

The ocean is very important to people. We eat food from the ocean. We travel across the ocean and live by its shores. Ocean algae make

The ocean affects our climate. Ocean water holds heat. The water flows to cooler parts of the world. It carries heat with it. The ocean makes the weather warmer in those places. Cold ocean water flows to other places on Earth. It cools the land there.

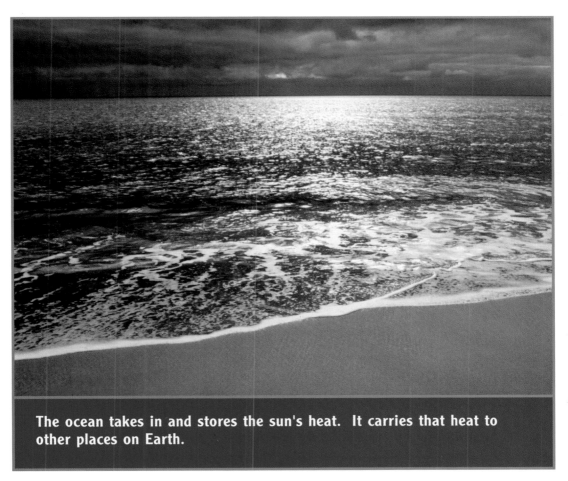

The ocean takes in and stores the sun's heat. It carries that heat to other places on Earth.

People build cities near the ocean. These cities have ports. Big ships come into the ports. These ships carry goods across the ocean. Ocean ports let people trade with faraway places.

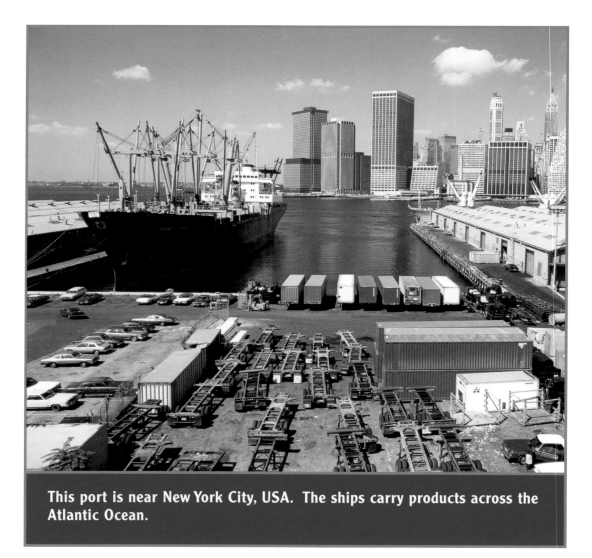

This port is near New York City, USA. The ships carry products across the Atlantic Ocean.

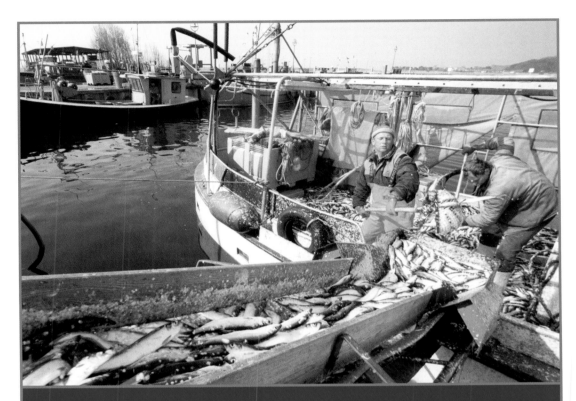

These fishermen have caught herring. People eat the fish and their eggs. Companies also use herring to make fish oils and animal feed.

People and their activities can harm ocean animals. There are lots of fish in the ocean. People catch fish to eat. Sometimes people catch too many fish from one place. These fish die out. Ocean animals that eat those fish must find other food.

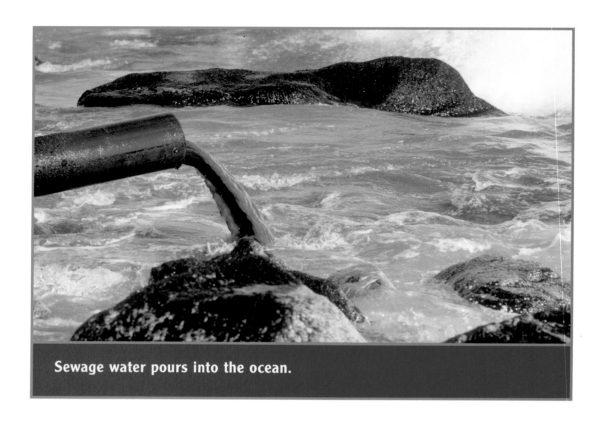
Sewage water pours into the ocean.

People can harm ocean water too. People put fertilizer on gardens or farmland. Fertilizer has nutrients. It helps plants grow. Sewage also has nutrients. Sewage is waste and water carried away in sewers and drains. Rain washes fertilizer and sewage into rivers. The rivers flow into the ocean. The nutrients from the land enter the sea.

The extra nutrients can make algae grow very fast. Algae cover the surface of the water. Then underwater plants cannot get enough light and may die.

Algae use the nutrients. When they die, bacteria feed on them. The extra bacteria use up oxygen in the water. Sea animals may not be able to get enough oxygen to breathe.

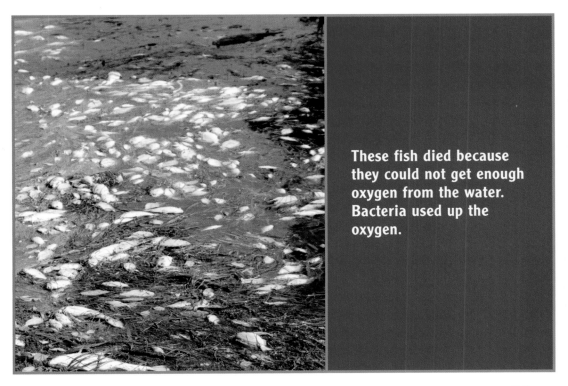

These fish died because they could not get enough oxygen from the water. Bacteria used up the oxygen.

The ocean is huge, but it is still harmed if we use it as a place to get rid of waste. Sea life dies if we dump waste in the ocean. People can work to keep fertilizer and sewage out of the ocean. We can also change the way we catch fish so that we don't take too many.

Rubbish on the beach or coastline can get washed into the water. Picking up the rubbish helps keep the ocean clean.

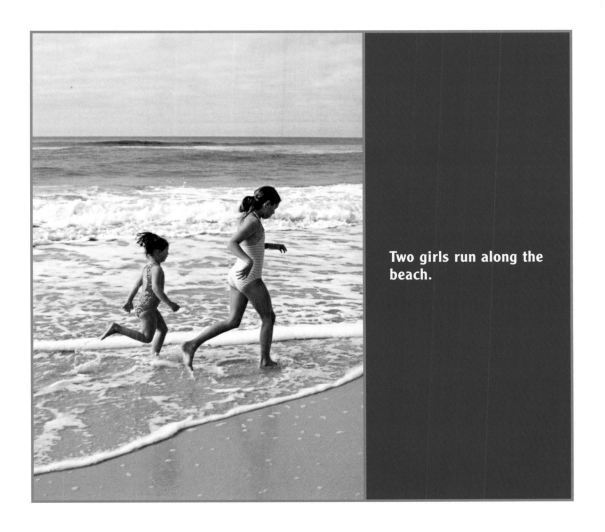

Two girls run along the beach.

People love to visit the ocean. We go to the beach. We swim and catch fish. But the ocean is more important than that. It gives us food. It gives us oxygen. It keeps our climate mild. We must take good care of the ocean environment.

A NOTE TO ADULTS
ON SHARING A BOOK

When you share a book with a child, you show that reading is important. To get the most out of the experience, read in a comfortable, quiet place. Turn off the television and limit other distractions, such as telephone calls. Be prepared to start slowly. Take turns reading parts of this book. Stop occasionally and discuss what you're reading. Talk about the photographs. If the child begins to lose interest, stop reading. When you pick up the book again, revisit the parts you have already read.

BE A VOCABULARY DETECTIVE

The word list on page 5 contains words that are important in understanding the topic of this book. Be word detectives and search for the words as you read the book together. Talk about what the words mean and how they are used in the sentence. Do any of these words have more than one meaning? You will find the words defined in a glossary on page 46.

WHAT ABOUT QUESTIONS?

Use questions to make sure the child understands the information in this book. Here are some suggestions:

> What did this paragraph tell us? What does this picture show? What is a food web? How do plants depend on animals? Where does energy in the ocean come from? What do we call animals that eat both plants and animals? How can people help to protect ocean plants and animals? What is your favourite part of the book? Why?

If the child has questions, don't hesitate to respond with questions of your own, such as What do *you* think? Why? What is it that you don't know? If the child can't remember certain facts, turn to the index.

INTRODUCING THE INDEX

The index helps readers find information without searching through the whole book. Turn to the index on page 48. Choose an entry such as *plants* and ask the child to use the index to find out how plants make their own food. Repeat with as many entries as you like. Ask the child to point out the differences between an index and a glossary. (The index helps readers find information, while the glossary tells readers what words mean.)

LEARN MORE ABOUT
OCEANS AND FOOD WEBS

BOOKS

Bailey, Jacqui. *Staying Alive: The Story of a Food Chain* (Science Works) A&C Black, 2006.

Laskey, Elizabeth. *Sea Turtles* (Sea Creature) Heinemann Library, 2003.

Lynch, Emma. *Ocean Food Chain* (Food Webs) Heinemann Library, 2005.

MacQuitty, Miranda. *Ocean* (Eyewitness Guide) Dorling Kindersley Publishers Ltd, 2003.

Marshall, Oliver. *Ocean* (Eye Wonder) Dorling Kindersley Publishers Ltd, 2004.

Pyers, Greg. *Ocean Explorer* (Habitat Explorer) Raintree, 2005.

Stille, Darlene R. *Octopuses* (Sea Creatures) Heinemann Library, 2003.

Theodorou, Rod. *To the Depths of the Ocean* (Amazing Journeys) Heinemann Library, 2006.

WEBSITES

BBC - GCSE Bitesize: Living Things
http://www.bbc.co.uk/schools/gcsebitesize/biology/livingthingsenvironment/1feedingrelationshipsrev1.shtml
This site has information on animals' feeding relationships and also looks at general food webs and food chains.

Ocean Living for Kids
http://nationalzoo.si.edu/Animals/OceanLiving/ForKids
Get the facts on seals and sea lions from the Smithsonian National Zoological Park website.

GLOSSARY

algae: water plants that use sunlight to make food. Some algae are tiny. Other algae, such as seaweeds, are large.

bacteria: tiny living things made of just one cell. Bacteria can be seen only under a microscope.

carnivores: animals that eat meat

consumers: living things that eat other living things. Animals are consumers.

decay: to break down

decomposers: living things that feed on dead plants and animals and break them down into nutrients

environment: a place where a creature lives. An ocean environment includes the air, water, sand or mud, weather, plants and animals in a place.

food chain: the way energy moves from the sun to a plant, then to a plant eater, then to a meat eater and finally to a decomposer

food web: many food chains connected together. A food web shows how all living things in a place need each other for food.

herbivores: animals that eat plants

nutrients: chemicals that living things need in order to grow

omnivores: animals that eat both plants and animals

photosynthesis: the way green plants use energy from sunlight to make their own food from carbon dioxide and water

plankton: small plants and animals that float in the ocean

producers: living things that make their own food. Plants are producers.

scavengers: animals that eat dead plants and animals

INDEX

algae 10, 14, 16–19, 20, 21,
    22–23, 29, 33, 36, 41

bacteria 5, 35, 41

carnivores 5, 24, 27

decomposers 9, 11, 12, 31–35, 41

energy moving through the ocean
    9–12, 20, 24

food chains and food webs 10–12

meat eaters 9, 11, 12, 19, 24–30

nutrients 5, 15, 31-32, 35, 40-41

omnivores 29–30

people and the ocean 36–43
photosynthesis 5, 14
plankton 5, 16, 21, 25, 27, 29, 30
plant eaters 9, 10, 11, 12, 17,
    20–23, 24
plants 8-11, 13–19, 24, 41
pollution 40–42
producers 5, 13, 16–17

scavengers 38

weather 8, 37, 43

First published in the United States of America in 2008.
Text copyright © 2008 by Lerner Publishing Group, Inc.